WIENER DOG ART
A FAR SIDE COLLECTION

WIENER DOG ART

A FAR SIDE COLLECTION

BY GARY LARSON

Futura

*The author would like to extend his thanks to Donna Pickert-Korris,
the extremely talented artist who did both the gray wash and
watercolor artwork on selected cartoons that appear in this book.*

A Futura Book

First published in the USA in 1990 by Andrews and McMeel
First published in Great Britain in 1991 by Futura Publications
a Division of Macdonald & Co (Publishers) Ltd
London & Sydney

1st Reprint 1991

Printed in Great Britain by
The Guernsey Press Company Limited, Guernsey, Channel Islands

ISBN 0 7088 4985 7

Futura Publications
A Division of
Macdonald & Co (Publishers) Ltd
165 Great Dover Street
London SE1 4YA

A Member of Maxwell Macmillan Publishing Corporation

It was very late, and Raymond, fighting insomnia, went for a midnight snack. Unfortunately, he never saw the duck blind.

"No *way* am I going to that party tonight!
I won't know anyone there, and that
means I'll be introduced
— *and you know I never learned how to shake!*"

"You eat what you've taken,
Mitchell....I know you're
just spreading it around."

"Well, here's your problem, Marge — if you and Bob really want kids, next time try sittin' on these little guys."

Special Agent Gumby falls into the frustrated hands of the enemy.

"On three, Vince. Ready?"

"Throw him in the swamp? You idiot! That's the *first* place they'll look."

Our protagonist is about to check on the progress
of her remodelers in this scene from
"Leona Helmsley Meets the Three Stooges."

And for the rest of his life, the young
reptile suffered deep emotional scars.

"This is no use, Wanda. It's like they say — we just
don't have lips."

"Henry! Our party's total chaos! No one knows
when to eat, where to stand, what to . . . .
Oh, thank God! Here comes a border collie!"

"Listen, Mom...I just wanted you to know I'm OK and the stampede seems about over — although everyone's still a little spooked. Yeah, I know...I miss the corral."

"And as amoebas, you'll have no problems recruiting other sales reps . . . just keep dividing and selling, dividing and selling."

And down they went: Bob and Francine — two more victims of the La Brea Carpets.

"Well, there he goes again.... 'Course, I guess
I did the same thing at his age — checking
every day to see if I was becoming a silverback."

"Wow, this place is really packed — or maybe it's
just my compound eyes."

Dog restaurants

Semi-desperadoes

Suddenly, a heated exchange took place between the king and the moat contractor.

"Well, there he is, Bobby — Big Red. Sure he's tough, but if you can ride him, he's yours."

Pirate manicures

Morning in the crypt

Studying the African bagel beetle

19

As a child, little Henry Jekyll would often
change himself into a big, red-haired
delinquent that parents in the neighborhood
simply dubbed "that Hyde kid."

"OK, Frank, that's enough. I'm sure the Jeffersons are quite amazed at your car headlight device."

For a very brief period, medieval
scientists were known to have dabbled
in the merits of cardboard armor.

"Excuse me...I know the game's
almost over, but just for the record,
I don't think my buzzer was working properly."

To his horror, Irving suddenly realized he had failed
to check his own boots before putting them on
just minutes ago.

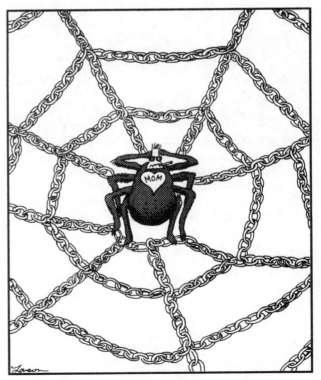

Tough spiders

"You ever do this? ... Just sit
in a place like this and antwatch?"

"You're so morbid, Jonathan — the paper comes,
and that's the first section you always head for."

"It's Vince, all right. It's his nose, his mouth, his fur ... but his eyes
— there's something not quite right about his eyes."

Ineffective tools of persuasion

"And one more thing about tomorrow's company picnic: Do I have to mention what happened last year when some wise guy sabotaged the games with a case of acid-filled LD-50s?"

"Why'd you do it, Biff? I mean, I always knew car chasing was in your blood — but the president's limo?"

Warren Hagstrom: Professional Western movie background street crosser

In the Chicken Museum

Suddenly, the door was kicked open,
and with nostrils flaring and manes flying,
wild horses dragged Sam away.

"Oh my God, Bernie! You're wearing my nylon?"

"Fellow octopi, or octopuses . . . octopi? . . . Dang, it's hard to start a speech with this crowd."

Ralph Harrison, king of salespersons

Suddenly, on a national talk show in front of
millions of viewers, Dick Clark ages 200 years
in 30 seconds.

The heart of the jungle now well behind them, the
three intrepid explorers entered the spleen.

Broca's brain, appendix, and baseball glove

Giraffe beach parties

"Farmer Bob.... Your barn door's open."

"So once they started talking, I just remained motionless, taking in every word. Of course, it was just pure luck I happened to be a fly on the wall."

Life among the clover

The parenting advantages of dentists

"Well, here we go, another exciting evening at the Murdocks', all of us sitting around going, 'Hello, my name is so-and-so....What's your name?...I wanna cracker. Hello, my name is so-and-so.'"

The deadly couch cobra — coiled and alert in its natural habitat

Wildlife day shifts

Carmen Miranda's family reunion

"And the really great thing about this jungle of ours
is that any one of you could grow up to be
King of the Apes."

Trouble brewing

March 16, 1942: The night before he leaves the Philippines, General MacArthur works on his farewell address.

"Listen, before we take this guy, let me ask you this: You ever kill a flea before, Dawkins? It ain't easy."

"You need to see medicine man — me just handyman."

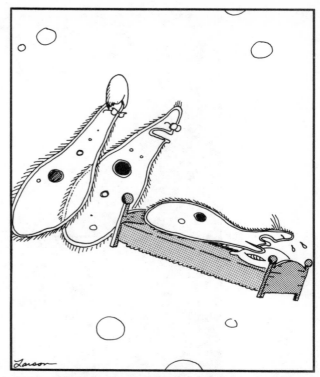

"Now Betty Sue, we know you're upset...breaking up with a boyfriend is always hard. But as they say, there are more protozoa in the lower intestine."

"Listen, you want to come over to my place?
I get great FM."

"For crying out loud, Patrick — sit down.
...And enough with the 'give me the potatoes or
give me death' nonsense."

"Well, here we go again.... Did anyone here *not* eat
his or her homework on the way to school?"

Darren's heart quickened: Once inside
the home, and once the demonstration
was in full swing, a sale was inevitable.

"All this time you've been able to go home
whenever you desired — just click your heels
together and repeat after me..."

Tragedy struck when Conroy, his mind preoccupied with work, stepped into the elevator — directly between a female grizzly and her cub.

"OK, Johnson — we've got a deal. We'll let your people and my people work out the details."

Competition in nature

**Becoming a rogue in his later years,
Dumbo terrorized the world's flyways.**

Early department stores

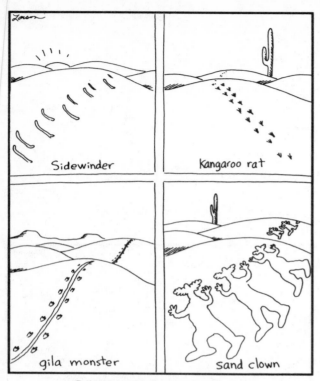

Common desert animal tracks

Bullknitters

Wiener Dog Art

Although seldom discussed in the writings of most art historians, the wiener dog (or dachshund, as at least twelve people still insist on calling it) was intermittently a favorite subject of many artists, including several of the Great Masters (although this remains controversial). In fact, throughout the history of mankind, the wiener dog has often been utilized as a symbol for many of our human traits: love, war, hunger, greed, fear, hypochondria, and swollen glands, to name just a few of the more common ones.

By way of example, the fear of wiener dogs, lytlelongdogophobia, was most prevalent in Mesopotamia around 500 B.C. and the art from this time reflected that culture's anxiety toward this little animal. Other societies, however, revered the canine, although we know little of these people since their civilizations lasted, on average, three to five weeks.

Why the wiener dog has found its way into our hearts and minds, and ultimately our culture, is difficult to say. We know only that, somehow, this small, sausage-shaped dog with its shrill, high-pitched bark and sometimes neurotic behavior has touched something we recognize deep inside ourselves.

Heretofore never published in book form, the following section represents a small but certainly sufficient glimpse into this little-known and unfortunately neglected area of art history.

Note: The author would like to thank the world's major collectors of wiener dog art (both of whom insisted on anonymity) for allowing their paintings to be reprinted herein.

Cave Art

Location: Southern France
c. 15,000 B.C.

In 1909, paleontologist Arnold Zimmerman stumbled across this Paleolithic cave painting in southern France. It is undoubtedly the earliest known form of wiener dog art, estimated to be around 17,000 years old. The drawing is a clear depiction of *Weenus giganticus*, commonly known as the woolly wiener dog—a creature that according to Professor Zimmerman, "must have struck utter terror in the hearts of primitive mail carriers."

Zimmerman's discovery ultimately brought him only grief, as other scientists began to question the legitimacy of this cave painting. (Special but inconclusive tests indicated the actual "paint" contained chemicals closely akin to a Magic Marker.) The controversy eventually ebbed, and Zimmerman moved on in his career to become a staunch supporter of Piltdown man.

Through the Storm

Artist: Boris Stromberg
64 x 64, oil on canvas
c. 1600

The Wienerkings (also known as Dachsmen) were aggressive, seafaring warriors who pestered European coastal villages in the eighth and ninth centuries. They were never known to actually kill anyone, but, instead, preferred to stab annoyingly at their victim's ankles. Perhaps even more interesting was their battle cry, described in some ancient legends as a "sort of yipping sound."

The Wienerkings vanished rather quickly, and historians are in dispute as to exactly why. The most prevalent theory, however, is that they may have repeatedly and inadvertently crossed paths with the Rottweilerites, another obscure people that just about everyone avoided.

The Bitches of Paradise

Artist: Bernardo Bartolini (Rubens school)
54 x 48, oil on canvas
c. 1608

The Renaissance saw the emergence of the "chunkified" wiener dog in the style of seventeenth-century Baroque art. Here, we see one such piece by Bernardo Bartolini (although he apparently preferred to sign his works with an informal "Bernie"). In 1612, Bernardo was commissioned to do a wiener dog fresco for King Giovanni D'Amento IV. Unfortunately, a revolt, led by a small clique of art critics, dethroned Giovanni—and Bernardo was arrested before he could begin his work. Giovanni was beheaded, and Bernardo was slapped around for a good five minutes and then released.

Wiener Dog with Head Turned

Artist: Pablo Picasso?
26 x 24, oil on canvas
1954

This is one of the more controversial works in this section. In 1986, this painting went on the auction block and a Japanese collector paid $38 million for what he believed was one of Picasso's startling interpretations of the wiener dog. Shortly thereafter, however, several experts came forth to challenge the painting's authenticity. New estimates now place the work's value somewhere between $14 and $22, most of that amount being attributed to the nice frame.

Bottle, Apple, Book, and Bowl of Wiener Dogs

Artist: Unknown
36 x 32, watercolor
1946

The wiener dog, especially in postwar Europe, was a frequent subject for still-life artists, almost to the point of cliché. Bowls of wiener dogs, baskets of wiener dogs, tubs of wiener dogs, dried wiener dogs, stuffed wiener dogs, and a myriad of other variations on this theme represented a quirky but strong artistic trend for seven and a half years. And then it stopped.

Runaways

Artist: Samuel J. Sullivan
28 x 22, oil on canvas
1896

In the latter part of the nineteenth century, wiener dogs were brought West in great herds by the backing of wealthy "wiener barons." These drives were occasionally enormous in scale, sometimes consisting of well over half a billion animals. There were two major routes (or "Wiener Trails") across the country, one starting in Boston and ending in San Francisco, the other starting in Chicago, circling that city several times (for greater momentum), dropping down to Dallas, back to Chicago (usually an error), down into New Mexico, and ending in what was then called Wienerville, Arizona (now an uninhabited area but renowned for its rich topsoil).

The artist, Samuel J. Sullivan, was still a young man in 1878 when he joined one of these expeditions, and here we see one of his action-filled paintings which captures a wienerboy at work. Sullivan reported that Indians never attacked these drives, believing the little dogs to be harbingers of bad luck. Indeed, there were few risks on a wiener trail, although we know from their songs and stories that wienerboys lived in a constant fear of ringworm.

The Persistence of Wiener Dogs

Artist: Salvador Dali?
24 x 20, oil on canvas
c. 1938

We have no conclusive proof that this is indeed the work of Salvador Dali, but we're pretty sure. The signature on the painting, believed to be a pseudonym, is actually "Labrador Dali," but most experts recognize (reluctantly) the unique stamp of the famous Spanish surrealist.

The Whine

Artist: Edvard Munch?
18 x 28, oil on canvas
1891

Once again, we have here a work in which the creator's identity technically remains a mystery, but whose disturbing, provocative use of the wiener dog practically screams, "Edvard, you veirdo you!"

This painting, along with a handful of other works by various artists, was stolen several years ago from one of New York's pretty good art museums. The brazen theft was a devastating blow to the art community. Interestingly enough, however, the very next day this particular painting was returned, found leaning against one of the museum's outside walls. According to the museum's curator at the time, the loss of all the works was an extreme offense, "but the return of 'The Whine' was absolutely the last straw."

Until finally being replaced by its more popular and deadly cousin, the Bowie spoon was often used to settle disputes in the Old West.

Inconvenience stores

The bozone layer: shielding the rest of the solar
system from the Earth's harmful effects.

"Rex! Don't take it! Everyone knows their mouths
are dirtier than our own!"

Randy Schueler and his wingless
butterfly collection

**Although it lasted only 2 million years, the
Awkward Age was considered a hazardous time
for most species.**

The rooster stared back at me, his power and confidence almost overwhelming. Down below, a female paused warily at the coop's entrance. I kept the camera running. They were beautiful, these "Chickens in the Mist."

"OK, Mr. Dittmars, remember, that brain is only a
temporary, so don't think too hard with it."

Deer Halloweens

Nerds of the Old West

"Well, here we go again! I *always* get the
gurney with one bad wheel."

"Oh, I don't know. Billy's been having trouble in school, and Sally's always having some sort of crisis. I tell you, Edith, it's not easy raising the dead."

The party had been going splendidly — and then Tantor saw the ivory keyboard.

The tragic proliferation of noseguns

"Don't worry...your little boy's somewhere
in our service department — but let's
move on and check out the TD500."

Tapeworms visiting a Stomach Park

Cow poetry

**Suddenly, second-chair granite rock's jealousy of
first-chair granite rock becomes uncontainable.**

"It's a fax from your dog, Mr. Dansworth. It looks like your cat."

"Wait a minute!...McCallister, you fool! *This* isn't what I said to bring!"

"Zorak, you idiot! You've mixed incompatible species in the earth terrarium!"

"For crying out loud, Igor! First there's
that screw-up with the wrong brain business,
and *now* you've let his head go through
the wash in your pants' pocket!"

"Oh my God! It's Leonard!...He's stuffed himself."

Wharf cows

Scene from *Dinner on Elm Street*

Ancient exterminators

Pinocchio in his later years

"This *must* be it, Jenkins — the
legendary Ugliest Place on Earth."

Scenes from classic nature films

"Our people are positioned on every street corner,
commander.... Shall we commence with our plan
to gradually eliminate these creatures?"

"Yes, yes, I *know* that, Sidney...*every*body knows *that!*... But look: Four wrongs *squared,* minus two wrongs to the fourth power, divided by this formula, *do* make a right."

Already concerned, Ernie watched in horror as one more elephant tried to squeeze on.

"Well, Mr. Rosenburg, your lab results look pretty good — although I might suggest your testosterone level is a tad high."

Runaway trains

"No doubt about it, boys. See these markings on the bottom? This
is an *Apache* pie pan!"

Scenes from the entomology underworld

"Roy, you get up on the hotel roof there — and for
godsakes, if you *are* plugged, don't just slump
over and die. Put some drama into it and throw
yourself screaming from the edge."

Practicing his skills wherever possible,
Zorro's younger and less astute brother,
Gomez, had a similar career cut short.

Daddy longleg jerks

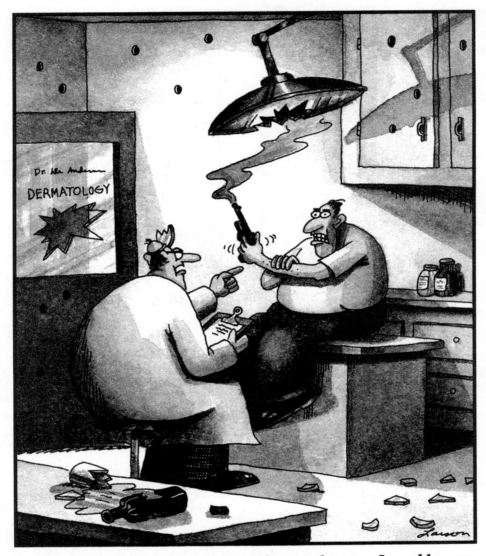

"First of all, Mr. Hawkins, let's put the gun down.... I would guess it's an itchy trigger finger, but I want to take a closer look."

Scene from the film *Giraffes IV:* This time, they're not just looking for acacia leaves.

Suburban headhunters

Times and places never to
insert your contact lens.

"Oh, no! I have several others — Oggy here is just
a tad aggressive, so he has to stay in a cage."

"Hey! What have I told you kids about screwing
around in front of that window?"

Punk accountants

Sheep health classes

When the monster came, Lola, like the
peppered moth and the arctic hare,
remained motionless and undetected.
Harold, of course, was immediately devoured.

**Thag Anderson becomes the first fatality as a result
of falling asleep at the wheel.**

Dinosaur nerds

"Well, I'm not sure.... I guess it's been washed."

Slug vacation disasters

"Well, that's an interesting bit of trivia —
I guess I *do* only dream in black and white."

After flicking on the light, Professor Zurkowitz is caught off guard by the overnight success of his efforts to crossbreed flying fish and piranhas.

Hours later, when they finally came to,
Hal and Ruby groggily returned to their
yard work — unknowingly wearing the radio
collars and ear tags of alien biologists.

"Man, Larry, I don't know if we're up to this.
I mean, this guy's got kneecaps from hell."

Convinced by his buddies that in actual fact they were only grave "borrowing," a young Igor starts on his road to crime.

"Dang! Every day, more and more swatters are movin' in."

"I say we do it ... and trichinosis be damned!"

"OK, Zukutu — that does it! Remember, those who live in grass houses shouldn't throw spears."

Bowlers' Hell

"Again? Why is it that the revolution always gets
this far and then everyone just chickens out?"

"Uh-oh. Carol's inviting us over for cake,
and I'm sure it's just *loaded* with palm oil."

Superman in his later years

Hibernating Eskimos

<u>INDEX</u>

X

Y

U

Z

V

W